Bliss

PRANAY

BUDDHA
WISDOM LIBRARY

Published by

FiNGERPRINT!
Prakash Books

Fingerprint Publishing
@FingerprintP
@fingerprintpublishingbooks
www.fingerprintpublishing.com

ISBN: 978 93 6214 207 8

Remembering our Buddha-nature
makes us joyful and blissful.

OM MANI PADME HUM

May joy fill the hearts of all beings,
May the shackles of suffering be broken,
May tranquility and unity reign supreme.
May my thoughts, words, and deeds
Radiate boundless love and compassion
For the well-being and happiness
Of all sentient beings,
Across the universe and beyond . . .

—A Buddhist Benediction

Naropa, look deep into the mirror of mind!
There dwell joy and bliss, eternal delight—
The secret abode of the Dakini!

—Tilopa's Mahamudra
Instructions to Naropa

Contents

1. Bliss through Buddhism   13

2. Ten Secrets for Happiness   19

3. The Buddha's Vision for Human Happiness   31

4. Zen Buddhism: Happiness in Tough Times!   35

5. Being Relaxed   39

6. Bhutan   43

7. It is All About Consciousness!   49

8. Mutual Respect   53

9. Be Like the Bee!   57

10. The Calm Mind   61

11. Neti, Neti!   65

12. Eureka Moments of Insight & Bliss!   67

13. Right Consciousness   71

14. Finding Joy in Simple Things   75

15. The Universe, Aliens & AI   79

16. The Blissful Energy of Buddhist Statues   83

17. The Simplicity of a Happy Attitude   87

18. Communicating Blissfulness   91

19. Being In Tune Within Yourself!   97

20. The Sahaj Path   101

21. The Warrior's Self-belief   103

22. The Question of Artificial Intelligence
    vs. Soulfulness   107

23. Focus vs. Awareness   111

24. Inner Power   113

25. The Whole Cosmos Has Consciousness!   117

26. Jiddu Krishnamurti and The Buddha   121

27. Physical Well-being   125

28. Moving toward Silence   127

29. Strengthening Yourself   129

30. Learn to Ignore Thoughts   133

31. The Principle of Emptiness   137

32. Be Detached from Hurt   139

33. Being Grounded in Happiness   141

34. Psychology   145

35. Withstanding Pain   147

36. The Inquisitive Mind   149

37. Nothing Can Confine Truth!   151

38. Materialism   153

39. Tranquility: The Way of the Mystic
    Warrior   155

40. You Do Not Have to Become Anything!   157

41. Have the Quality of the Lotus   159

42. Aapo Deepo Bhava   161

43. Simplicity Creates Great Things   163

44. Being Choiceless   165

45. Evolution   167

46. Finding True Purpose in Life   169

47. Mind–Body–Spirit Balance   171

48. The Power of Compassion   173

49. The Buddha's Mystic Philosophy   175

50. The Most Valuable Lessons   177

51. Buddhism's 'Ten Perfections' for
    Enlightened Bliss   179

Acknowledgments   185

CHAPTER 1

Bliss through Buddhism

The peaceful live happily.

Gautam Buddha

No individual in history has bestowed as many teachings to manifest true bliss as has the great Gautam Buddha. He used to say, "Bliss is attainable by everyone who walks the noble path"!

In Buddhism, the idea of bliss (*Ananda* or *Sukha*) is one where we achieve a state of mental, physical, and spiritual tranquility. This tranquility makes us expand ourselves and free ourselves. It puts us deeper into a state of pure witnessing or meditativeness. That way, we find an inherent joy welling up within us. We become naturally full of happiness. Such natural happiness is the bedrock of Buddha's teachings.

A famous prayer in Tibetan Buddhism says, "May all auspiciousness and goodness increase. May all beings be endowed with happiness and its causes. May all be free from suffering and its causes. May all never be separated from the sacred happiness that is free from suffering."

THE BUDDHA'S PATH

Gautam Buddha's journey—from a life of luxury, to complete renunciation, to understanding the nature of suffering and discovering the path to true joy—makes him an unparalleled teacher for all beings.

The Buddha's approach amalgamates mysticism, psychology, science, and spirituality to comprehend sorrow and attain bliss. Buddhism offers insights into finding inner peace and understanding existence.

Buddha taught mindfulness, meditation, and recognizing our inherent bliss and Buddha-nature (*Buddha-dhatu*). He guides us in dealing with thoughts and emotions to find genuine happiness and extend kindness to others. His message emphasizes harmony and interconnectedness beyond selfishness. Buddha's practical and profound teachings show us how to create inner peace and connect with others.

Throughout human history, millions of people have drawn deep inspiration from Buddha's example to help discover their inner bliss and happiness.

THE BUDDHIST PERSPECTIVE

According to the Buddha's perspective, happiness resides within us and should not rely on external factors. When the mind is tranquil and detached from desires and attachments, genuine contentment and joy emerge naturally. Clinging to things restricts our joy, but by relaxing this clinging, we can attain lasting happiness and ultimate spiritual liberation, known as *Nirvana* (*Nibbana* in the Buddha's language of Pali). The Buddha looked at human sorrow and happiness from infinite dimensions, including psychological and mystical levels. Buddha is a mentor who teaches the art of finding joy in life. His timeless methods and findings cover a wide range of topics, including psychotherapy, neurology, spiritual ecstasy, and enlightenment—and every other angle that human consciousness can think of! Buddha's teachings have special relevance because they perfectly align with modern medical research on the mind and provide empirical evidence of human joy. Buddha's wisdom is still relevant today as it aligns perfectly with current medical research on the mind and empirical evidence of human happiness.

The subject of *Ananda,* or blissful delight, was very close to the Buddha's heart. His closest disciple was his cousin 'Ananda'—it was Buddha's monastic name for him. Buddha believed that mankind's search for happiness is the basis of life itself. We can encapsulate the gist of Buddhism's teachings for happiness or *Ananda* within specific key points (as has been done in the subsequent chapters of this book). These key points or principles are based on the core Indian Buddhist texts, as Buddha spent the entirety of his monastic life in India: it is always good to go back to the original Pali language scriptures, as that was the language he used.

By aligning with Buddhist principles like mindfulness (*Sati* in Pali), meditation (*Jhāna*), and ethical behavior (*Śīla*), we uncover the wellspring of bliss within ourselves. This leads to profound contentment, well-being, and spontaneous fulfillment, which constitutes true happiness. Unlike materialistic pursuits, this happiness is not contingent on external factors like wealth or power; instead, it emanates from our inner joy, integration, empathy, and compassion. Such happiness is enduring and robust, representing genuine happiness from the Buddhist viewpoint. These principles are echoed in Buddhist paths worldwide: Tibetan, Burmese, Sri Lankan, Thai, Chinese, Japanese, Mongolian, etc.

CHAPTER 2

Ten Secrets for Happiness

Sabbe Satta Sukhi Hontu
(May all beings be happy!)

The ten secrets or root principles distilled from Buddha's teachings and Buddhist wisdom are as follows:

1. ABSOLUTE CALMNESS

The idea of being completely calm and tranquil (*Passadhi* in Pali) is the root of true bliss in the Buddhist vision. Without tranquility in mind, calmness, and inner peace (*Santi* in Pali), happiness is an impossibility.

The Buddhist attitude of Samatha, the meditative vision of looking at life with a complete calmness of demeanor in heart and mind, is the basis upon which we must understand the pursuit of happiness or joy in life. It is all about finding happiness through the inner quietness of being. That is real happiness. Without inner quietness, there is no taste of higher happiness.

The happiness that arises from inner quietness is free of external circumstances and not dependent on any material circumstance.

Ordinarily, what we consider happiness is temporary enjoyment; it is not abiding happiness. It mostly depends on something happening in the material world: when we succeed at something, accomplish something, and so on. But Buddha is talking about the happiness of finding the light of tranquil joy within oneself.

Through calmness comes truth; through calmness comes happiness. Once the restlessness within the mind is settled, happiness or bliss arises.

2. KEEP MOVING FORWARD!

The second secret is related to the ancient mystic formula that the Buddha used to give his disciples: "*Charaiveti, Charaiveti*"— Keep moving forward, never look back!

The attitude of such dynamism in life—when your mind does not keep returning to what happened yesterday—determines happiness outcomes.

If your mind keeps going back to what has already happened, you can often become anxious, entrapped by thinking, and colored by previous stresses. Leave all that behind! They create confusion, not clarity.

The possibility of higher happiness or blissful joy arises only by boldly and dynamically moving on.

3. BOTH, PATH & DESTINATION!

The third secret is based on Buddha's words: "There is no path to happiness. Happiness itself is the path!"

Buddha emphasizes a fundamental truth: happiness should not be viewed as something to be attained in the future or upon achieving specific goals. Instead, wherever you find yourself, in whatever circumstances, be happy. You will naturally move toward greater happiness if you find joy in walking the path. The destination, too, will become one of bliss. But if, while walking the route itself, you are not happy, then nothing will fulfill you.

The concept of discovering the all-blissful higher self or Buddha within you in this present moment, wherever you are, and whatever situation you are in is fundamental in the Buddha's eyes. It emphasizes the significance of life's quality over material outcomes. Buddha's approach is to appreciate what you already have. Through this mindset, your inner being is lit with the intelligence of more incredible bliss and delight.

4. RIGHT THOUGHT

The fourth is based on Buddha's consciousness teachings. He tells us: "We are formed and molded by our thoughts. Those whose minds are shaped by noble thoughts give happiness when they speak or act. Happiness follows them like a shadow that never leaves."

Here, Gautam Buddha is talking about how the natural nobility of our consciousness determines how much bliss we can move toward. Pay attention to your consciousness. Nurture it with good thoughts. And then, happiness is yours. Do not diminish your consciousness through fear and trepidation.

5. MEDITATIVENESS

The Buddha always emphasized the meditative attitude toward life, which is the very root of understanding the infinite bliss and happiness of which one is capable. He said: "The enlightened one intent on *Jhāna* (meditation) should find delight in the forest, practice Jhāna at the foot of a tree, attaining his happiness."

Here, Buddha talks about *Jhāna* in the Pali language and *Dhyaana* in Sanskrit—the meditative aspect of life.

Now, we have to remember that Buddhism is both deep and realistic. When Buddha talks about meditating in the forest, we are not to take it literally; these days, that is a very difficult task.

Yet what he is emphasizing is that we are not to leave any opportunity to be meditative. Act on your meditative impulses in whatever moments you have. We do not know how long we are going to survive. We do not know about tomorrow. But if you rest your consciousness in meditation, remember that blissful delight, joy, and happiness will follow as a natural consequence. That is the most fundamental point.

The meditative state helps you release the energy force usually held back within you. It helps your innate spiritual and psycho-spiritual energies find creative expression, which leads to bliss.

6. SHARING

Buddha says: "Thousands of candles can be lit from a single candle, and the candle's life will not be shortened. Happiness never decreases by being shared."

Here, Buddha talks about his most important teachings related to sharing, a friendly attitude, and the concept of *Maitri*. The idea of Maitri implies being a friend to the entire world. The future Buddha is stated to be the Maitreya Buddha.

The idea is that you have to share the best energies that you have. And there is nothing better than sharing your joy. When you share this joyful bliss or ananda, it increases not only for the other but also for you. So that is a wonderful thing. If we remember that, then not only do we spontaneously become valuable to others in the world, but we also remove the thorns in our mental processes. Our anxieties are released due to wanting to share our ananda with others. This very impulse makes every moment a more joyous one.

Never hesitate to share moments of joy with others. And it does not necessarily mean a person. It could be sharing your joy with nature. The point is this: share your bliss with the world, with the people you work with, the people you are in personal relationships with, and even with relative strangers. Sharing is the key thing. The idea is to become a vibration and energy of sharing. That is the very secret of Maitreya and a very deep secret for generating happiness.

7. CREATION OF VALUE

The seventh thing we ought to note about Buddhism and happiness is the idea of creating value. Buddha says, "Happiness comes when both your words and your work are of value to yourself and others."

Here, Buddha talks about the state of speech, thought, and action, whereby you can awaken your own nobility and higher virtues. Be a value-creator for others. In ways small or big, try to benefit others. That benefits your own being. It leads to value creation within your own being.

This principle is behind the whole law of Karma, the law of reciprocal action. Send out your good actions and thoughts into the world, send out good words and impulses into the world, and you get it back manifold. It is the very underlying key of the reciprocal law of life. What you sow is what you reap!

Create your life with a focus on creating value for others. And that can happen in many ways. That can happen through empathy. It can occur through compassion. It can happen by doing something tangible, yet even the so-called intangible has value. Even the very effort to say to yourself, "I am going to be somebody who is a force of good in the world," resolves your attitude toward others and the world, and goes from negativity to value-creation. Thereby sparking off a process of greater happiness within you.

8. VIRTUE

The eighth secret is about the practice of virtue. Buddha says: "Set your heart on doing good; do it over and over again, and you will be filled with greater happiness."

Buddhism is all about practice. Practicing virtue is, in fact, a consistent theme throughout Buddhist teachings, starting with the direct root teachings of Buddha in India and being transmitted through the Theravada Buddhism of Sri Lanka, Mahayana Buddhism of Japan, Vajrayana Buddhism of Tibet, Zen Buddhism of Japan, and so on.

The idea of practicing virtue is self-explanatory and is bound to lead us to greater happiness. It is, in fact, the very basis for changing our outlook from anxiety-oriented to happiness-oriented. The good Buddhist is happiness-oriented and is himself of good cheer, spreading this cheer to all in one's environment.

9. LETTING GO

The ninth secret has to do with letting go of all things holding you back. Do not get stuck by any burdens of regretful feelings. Buddha says: "It is like things that happiness arises in a person who is free from guilt or remorse."

In other words, Buddha is telling us to leave aside those emotions which have held us mentally captive. Let go of those energies that have been shrinking your consciousness, making you narrower and uncreative. The greatest shrinkage of consciousness happens through remorse, regret, and remembrance of failures. Leave all that; there is no perfection in the world as such! The only perfection is the state of Ananda, the state of bliss. And that is in your hands!

Be established in bliss. Do not worry about what you can and cannot do in life.

This idea of mental and emotional release liberates, taking one several steps closer to enlightenment or Nirvana, which is Buddhism's ultimate aim.

10. THE MOMENT

The tenth secret is being established at the moment. Buddha says: "Do not dwell upon the past. Do not dream about the future. Focus your consciousness on the present moment."

This point is the real crowning glory of Buddhism. It tells us that while the ego invests its energy in the past or the future, our true self-nature is always situated in the moment. Identification with one's greater happiness through understanding one's self-nature or 'Buddha nature' implies a change in your attitude from past or future-oriented to becoming moment-oriented. Then, all the most vital energies within you become integrated into one singular, blissful force and dynamic power!

CHAPTER 3

The Buddha's Vision for Human Happiness

The Buddha and his vision are essential for the world today because he bridges the Eastern world and the Western world. He is a symbol of universality. In a globalized world, he is the ultimate symbol of somebody whose view can encompass all viewpoints. He is truly beyond any particular boundary or

31

narrow ideology. He takes us toward a vision where we have no limitations of caste, creed, nationality, etc. And understanding this universality of the Buddha is very important for achieving happiness and bliss in life.

While the Buddha is ancient, his wisdom resonates with the most modern findings in neuroscience and cosmology. Over the last few decades, much research has been done into Buddhist techniques for well-being. And it has been found on brain-mapping and neurological tests that these create a feeling of true wellness. From Buddha's *Vipassana* and *Anapanasati* meditations to his ideas of human dynamism (the idea of flow, moving forward dynamically, *Charaiveti Charaiveti*, as he used to tell his disciples), we can find that he indeed gifts us with the gift of well-being from within.

We become more open and accepting when we unburden ourselves from the world's limiting ideologies and align ourselves with the Buddha's energy of complete openness of mind and heart. This very openness raises us both to a level of spiritual consciousness and to the level of being more productive and better value-creators within the world.

There is a reason so much of Japanese management theory is based upon the Buddha's teachings. The idea of finding and being connected with the silence of your being, the idea of unlocking the inner power of Buddhahood within you—all things that allow us to move toward a more positive, futuristic vision for ourselves and those we serve in the world.

No matter what one is doing—whether one is in technology, or is a businessperson, a team worker, or a leader—Buddha's teachings because they are based upon self-truth, imbue us with the ultimate power to create self-happiness and happiness for others!

CHAPTER 4

Zen Buddhism: Happiness in Tough Times!

Some of Gautam Buddha's most fundamental teachings concern how to face tough times, difficult situations, challenges, and crises in life. We can examine Zen Buddhism of Japan to see the Buddha's best teachings regarding crisis situations.

You see, Japanese culture has an exciting take on crises. The Japanese have been buffeted by many crises over the millennia: multiple earthquakes, tsunamis, etc. Yet, a few spiritual fundamentals have kept them very strong and spirited in the face of these crises. They are the best example of people striving for bliss even amidst challenges.

Zen Buddhism is the ultimate flowering of Japanese culture. It plays a very important part in it. It emphasizes the cultivation of stoicism and courage in navigating life's challenges. Stoicism itself is a Greek philosophy but has parallels with Zen. But Zen is uniquely profound because it teaches you the idea of non-reactivity: do not react hastily to situations, have patience within your being, and settle your consciousness within your being. Then happiness, bliss, and excellence arise automatically.

In Zen, it is said that our consciousness is like the water flowing in a stream. If you disturb that stream, all the mud at the bottom of the stream will muddy the water. We need to bring our being into such a state of smooth flow that the water is crystal clear and flowing. Do not disturb the consciousness. Rather, bring the consciousness to a state of utter silence. That is what the Japanese Zen meditation called 'Zazen' is. It means simply sitting silently, not doing anything. It is about settling yourself within your own innate power. That allows you to find the luminous aspects of yourself, your self-bliss, and all of existence. And so doing, you are lit with your own inner light, your own inner courage, your own inner happiness, and inner wisdom, even in the face of crises and challenges.

This allows you to function optimally when most needed and takes you toward true bliss!

CHAPTER 5

Being Relaxed

The different schools of Buddhism teach various things. Yet, one principle that they all teach is being inwardly relaxed.

Over the centuries, Buddhism evolved into its various regional aspects. There is Sri Lankan Buddhism, Burmese Buddhism, Tibetan Buddhism or Vajrayana/Tantric Buddhism, the Mahayana Buddhism of

China, the Zen Buddhism of Japan, the Buddhism of Thailand, Laos, Cambodia, Vietnam, Mongolia, and so on. Yet, they are all bound together by a common insistence on cultivating a relaxed inward being, a cool calmness within oneself.

The Buddha's message is to be inwardly quiet, inwardly unshaken, contented, and collected. Life seems much easier if you can be truly relaxed, collected, and integrated inwardly. Its various challenges can be faced with equipoise and confidence. Don't let any outer circumstances create emotional turmoil within you. No matter what happens, be relaxed and silent within your being. There is no need to respond verbally or with abusive actions to negativity from the outside.

The real spiritual heart is one that is so powerful that it is both meek and peace-loving but, at the same time, truly strength-oriented! It seeks to build on the higher strengths of our human consciousness. And when we build on our higher strengths, we automatically become happier and more blissful. The higher strength of human consciousness lies in the nobler part of ourselves: empathy, compassion, love, concern, creativity, and so on.

Do not get bound by the lower. At the core of Buddhism lies the ability to be comfortable within your own being, regardless of the circumstances. This unshakable inner peace is cultivated through the practice of meditation and mindfulness, enabling individuals to maintain a state of profound calmness and serenity. This teaching of Buddha finds particular resonance in Taoism and Buddhism's Japanese avatar of Zen. The ability to be in an inward rhythm and enjoy the melody of life, no matter what storm comes your way . . . this is highly important!

There is always an inward melody of life! Learn to pay heed to that. There is always a light of being available to us. We just need to internalize enough to realize that light of being and thereby become blissful.

CHAPTER 6

Bhutan

Namo Amitabha Buddha
Om Ami Dewa Hri
(Mantric invocation to the Amitabha
Buddha, said to shower happiness,
liberation, and manifestation in the
pure land of bliss (Sukhavati).)

The beautiful Buddhist country of Bhutan, set amidst the Himalayas, believes in the concept of *Gross National Happiness* (GNH). This is a profoundly important index that they have created and it has been appreciated worldwide. Based on Buddhist principles, the Bhutanese idea is that the true measure of success is inward happiness and bliss.

Yes, *GDP* or *Gross Domestic Product* signifies material value creation. But eventually, the true way to success is to create happiness for oneself and for one's environment. That is why, in Bhutan, much attention is given to the environmentally sound approach to life.

It is all about taking an intuitive, happy, and meditative approach to whatever we do. That way, we become more wholehearted and tremendously spiritual and bring a powerful energy of fulfillment to all the tasks that we attempt.

People over the millennia in India have attested to this. In fact, the greatest kings in India have been said to manifest this intuitively meditative approach to life. It creates well-being and happiness for all. One example is Chandragupta Maurya, the great king who actually renounced his kingdom in his early 40s to become a Jain monk. His descendant, Ashoka the Great, is another. Ashoka's values were, of course, imbibed directly from Buddhism. Both these people have become legends when it comes to kingship and leadership simply because they could manifest this quality of meditativeness in their lives.

Similarly, we have the example of the great avatar Ram, the archetype of the universal hero; he is the protagonist in India's epic, the Ramayana. Remember, the Ramayana is not restricted to Hindu countries. In Thailand, a Buddhist country, the kings are still called Rama after Ram. Similarly, in Cambodia, the Ramayana is known as the 'Reamker' and is celebrated in Bali, Indonesia, in its more Hindu connotations.

Ram remained inwardly blissful, in the state of deep *Ananda*, in even the toughest circumstances in life. No matter what challenges he faced, he maintained his inward integrity. And that makes him a legend, a truly successful leader. So, for us to shine in our own lives and work, whether we are in leadership positions or not, we must carry the spirit of meditative *Ananda* within ourselves and in all that we do.

In Indian thought, the essential need of the human being is not described as the search for physical pleasure, that which can be found in sex, good food, enjoyment, and so on. No! The essential search of all beings is said to be a desire for happiness. That is the ultimate desire for all of us, whether we believe it or not. Yet, our idea is that we can find happiness in other things. But the material does not take us to higher happiness.

Manifesting a joyful attitude within ourselves in the midst of all that we do is really both the path and the aim of the Buddhist way. There is no difference between the path and the aim of happiness. Walk the first step with happiness, and you are already there, moving toward the destination, which is that of greater happiness.

So, make your steps and your destination synchronous, give them the same energy of happiness, and then you will find that not only does your work become more harmonious, but your relationships at work also become more harmonious. You are able to become a carrier of happiness and share happiness with others.

Gautam Buddha used to say that happiness sharing is the greatest virtue! Happiness shared does not diminish our vastness of happiness—it increases it manifold. Hence, follow that example in all matters.

CHAPTER 7

It is All About Consciousness!

Buddhism is unique because it talks about human consciousness or *Chetana* itself. Its teachings are not overly 'religious.' It tells us how to better our consciousness to confront and surmount human problems, thereby moving toward pure bliss.

The Buddha was a most prolific and efficient teacher. He devised many means and teachings for people to put their energy into attaining spiritual truth and happiness and, on the other hand, how to live a balanced life in the middle of all life situations. His teachings are never extreme. That is why his teachings are called the 'middle path.'

His teachings seem extremely rational, sane, and logical because they do not require any blind belief or faith. In that way, Buddhism is highly different from world religions. Yet, in a way, it encapsulates the greatest teachings of Indian civilization for thousands of years: the teachings of the Upanishads and the Vedas, the teachings of Vedanta philosophy, and the teachings of the Jain Tirthankaras. Buddha is regarded as the ninth avatar in Indian mythology. And he is truly a symbol of the state of consciousness which Indic religions have professed to be the ideal state of realization and bliss, within which both material and spiritual aspects of life are intertwined.

The Buddha used to say that it is essential for us to take a wholesome approach to mind, body, and spirit. All three are to be held in a great state of balance. He used to say, "Health is the greatest wealth." This is especially relevant when confronted by so many different kinds of microbes and world-threatening diseases.

So it's all about the balance of mind-body-spirit. Buddhism teaches us that it is essential for us to live lives of physical, mental, emotional, and spiritual balance.

Buddha emphasized living with purity on the physical plane. Paying attention to what you eat and drink is the first step. If you can do that, you will attain natural joy. The body strengthens its immunity, becoming prepared to take on the onus of human life. Avoid hankering after everything that tempts you.

CHAPTER 8

Mutual Respect

We have heard of the old saying that we should treat others as we wish to be treated. In Buddhism, this is not just a saying; it is *a living philosophy*. The idea of Buddhism is to have *mutual respect* with fellow beings.

Mutual respect implies empathy, a feeling that whatever you do to others comes back and echoes in you.

You must nourish others with your good energies. Remembering this makes half our problems in life disappear. Often, we send out negative vibes into the world. The way of Buddhism is to share all that is best within you. Then, people are automatically attracted to your aura, to that invisible vibe and attitude that you broadcast from your being.

Most of our communication is non-verbal. It is all about our intrinsic energy. That is why you will notice that when some people enter a room, you feel perfect, even if they do not say anything; if others do, you may feel a negative feeling. It is all about that innate quality of being that we constantly transmit into the world. If you make that suitable, all your human interactions will go right. Then, even if someone has not been kind to you in the past, you will see that they will have a positive attitude toward you.

This idea is illustrated by a story about the Buddha: one day, a man came and spat at him during one of his discourses to his *Sangha* or commune. The disciples wanted to beat up that man. But Buddha simply wiped the spit from his face. The next day, the person felt so bad that he came, apologized to the Buddha, and became a follower. The Buddha told his disciples that a person of true intelligence never reacts to negativity; a person always acts out of the best feeling. And then, that feeling is reciprocated by the universe.

The known story of the Indian God Krishna also illustrates this idea. One day, he was sitting with his wife Rukmini at his palace in Dwarka when he suddenly rushed toward the door at lunch. But then he paused a moment and came back. Rukmini was puzzled. She said: "Lord, why did you rush toward the door and then just come back? I could not understand." He said: "You know, there is a disciple of mine who lives very far away, and I saw that he's in distress. People were abusing him, and I needed to go to his aid." But then Rukmini said: "Lord, why didn't you go?" He said: "No, by that time, my disciple had picked up stones, and he started pelting stones at those people who insulted him. He did a negative act, so he did not need me. All would have been well if he had just been patient and called upon the divine being within him. But he chose to respond negatively."

So, remember, it is always about sending out positive vibes into the world, which truly matters. And it is simply a question of attitude! Cultivate this attitude in all your day-to-day activities. Then, you will see that half your worries and half your distresses in life disappear because you are not reactive. You become truly awakened and active in your responses. You act out of your highest self. When you act out of your highest self, the flow of bliss and happiness follows as a natural consequence.

CHAPTER 9

Be Like the Bee!

In Buddhism, the most significant value in life is sharing and spreading *Ananda* or bliss through one's work. It is said that we are to do all our work as if we are flowing in a great current of river water— unattached, free, pure, and happy. In Indian philosophy, in general, honeybees are taken as the ultimate example of *Ananda* and great happiness, shared and spread through work!

You see, honeybees work in a great spirit of rapture, exuberance, bliss. They do their work in a great spirit of dynamic happiness, but at the same time, their happiness helps the nectar be created! The bee helps pollinate all the flowers and all the trees. Interestingly, modern science tells us that the most exciting species on earth, if it has to be chosen, would be the honeybee because their whole function in ecology is priceless; their work is priceless! Should honeybees become extinct, Nature will suffer immensely because pollination, foliage, and fruitage will not happen. The whole ecology, the whole ecosystem, the whole environment will be destroyed.

The work of the honeybees is so essential. Their work always happens in a state of supreme rapture, exuberance, and bliss. They are cooperating. They help each other. They are assisting plants to help different species, and through this whole cycle, they're setting into motion great events that benefit the entire earth. So, the tiny work of one honeybee- that bee could be a simple worker bee, or it could be the queen bee, or it could be the guard bee, who guards the beehive and protects the honey, and so on- it could be in any capacity, is exceedingly powerful!

It teaches that each one of us can create something valuable through our work, which goes beyond us and is more significant than us. That is the secret of success at work. It truly means working through the principle of *Ananda* or supreme happiness!

The Calm Mind

When the mind is calm, it automatically connects with bliss. This lesson is at the heart of Buddha's formula for truly successful and happy living.

Cultivate that inner light of calmness that already exists within your being. It implies being inwardly cool. Then, you can do everything that you deal with in a cool manner. If you are agitated and anxious, the whole world looks like your enemy. The whole world seems difficult to deal with.

The Buddhas understood that we must recognize the divine spark of Buddhahood within ourselves. That automatically creates calmness and, thereby, bliss within us. Make that the very basis of your life. Then, you develop the guts to face up to any difficult situation in life, no matter what. You develop root-level mental strength, charisma, natural leadership traits, decision-making clarity, and so on.

Know that within you, your consciousness is pure, divine, and intrinsically calm, the witness of all things! Do not identify yourself by body and mind. You are pure consciousness itself. Cut your idea of unhappiness with the sword of true knowledge, saying to yourself, "I am pure consciousness; I am also a Buddha deep within!" This creates the consciousness to go past your limitations, inhibitions, and fears. You stop being afraid.

Our biggest problem in life is that we become fearful of things, which inhibits our capacity for bliss and happiness. Replace fear with calmness and coolness, and you will see that you feel the serenity and dynamism of being. You feel the arising of wisdom within you. And where these things are, undisturbed bliss follows spontaneously.

You are an integral part of universal consciousness. Knowing this, feel calm and relaxed within. Calmness and coolness create true inspiration and unlock our highest intelligence. In the Buddhist view, there is a supreme consciousness behind universal energy at work, which is also within us as our Buddha seed. The most destructive way to look at life is that we think we are limited in scope. We forget that we have the Buddha seed within us.

Knowing oneself as pure consciousness and absolute calmness, one moves toward that which is called Enlightenment or *Nirvana* in Buddhism. In Hinduism, a similar concept is called *Mukti* or *Moksha-* complete freedom. Complete freedom means freedom from fear, freedom from the idea that you are agitated and anxious. You can never indeed lose that seed of Buddhahood because it is your self-nature.

Establishing yourself in yourself-nature, you move toward a super-conscious way of purposeful living. You move toward what in Hinduism has been called the state of *Sat-Chit-Ananda*: truth, higher consciousness, and ultimate bliss. Go beyond your ordinary way of looking at things, the complexes we have. Have empathy for life and have self-respect and self-dignity.

Ultimately, we are not the *doers* in life. There is a great power through which everything moves. Once you realize that higher principles govern us, and that also exist within us, all anxiety is removed. We can come to a complete calmness. Always know within yourself that you have an inner richness of the Buddha seed that is completely calm, serene, and dynamizes you to succeed and become blissful in your own field of life.

CHAPTER 11

Neti, Neti!

There is a story about a sculptor who was asked how he creates his beautiful works of art. He thought about it for a second and said, "I only look at the piece of stone, and I chip away at that which is not required. Then what is left is the sculpture." And this, in a nutshell, explains the Buddha's attitude to life. He used to talk about *Neti Neti* and the way of negation.

Chip away at all that is not needed or essential, and you will be left with pure truth.

In the West, over the last century, there has been a lot of emphasis on positive thinking. But Buddha's way was to negate and eliminate most concepts in life. It is not enough to be positive. Positivity sometimes clouds our minds with too many preconceptions. The way of *Neti Neti* is the sword of discrimination, that which is called *Viveka*. It helps us get rid of the excess baggage in life. That excess baggage could be in the form of how we spend our time, our relationships, how we work, and so on.

So, the essential lesson from this is that we should be minimalistic. We are to cut down our thoughts, we are to cut down our desires, we are to cut down our clinging to things. With that cutting down, what is left is pure truth, pure consciousness, and pure bliss.

CHAPTER 12

Eureka Moments
of Insight & Bliss!

We have all heard the story about Archimedes discovering his principle of buoyancy and exclaiming, 'Eureka!' Eureka moments are breakthrough moments of creativity and insight. From the point of view of Buddhism, true insight or Pragya happens when our level of consciousness is completely clear, blissful, and in a state of flow, immersed in its own self-bliss.

The word 'eureka' and the exclamation it implies signifies great ecstasy or *Ananda*. And that is how we must prepare ourselves if we want to be truly creative. In all creative fields, no matter what you do, whether you are a musician, a designer, a programmer, or an artist, you must keep your consciousness prepared for creative breakthroughs.

We can look at Albert Einstein. He used to prepare himself for insights and creativity by playing his favorite music on the violin—that of Bach and Mozart. Einstein used to go as far as to say that without Bach and Mozart, he would never have been who he was. The music used to put him in an ecstatic frame of mind and trigger his sparks of creativity through his thought experiments.

Hence, the ancient emphasis of the sages on immersing our consciousness in its own self-bliss or Ananda is key when it comes to creating insightful and innovative situations through our activities; these could be work-related, relationship-related, and so on. A somber or dull attitude does not trigger a higher truth, higher creativity, or higher innovativeness.

Truly disruptive thinkers and charismatic leaders in business have this quality: you will notice that Richard Branson of Virgin Group always seems to give off a great vibe of happiness to those he interacts with. With Elon Musk, you would see that there is an underlying joy within him when he is interacting with people. Hence, the principle of blissful consciousness is important. It catalyzes our work.

CHAPTER 13

Right Consciousness

The Buddha said that right consciousness is the foundation of doing things right in life. And what is proper consciousness? It implies consciousness which is like water: water can fill any vessel and take any shape. In other words, proper consciousness is that which is so clear and pure that it can respond perfectly well to every situation in life.

Right consciousness implies the consciousness that is imbued with wisdom, goodness, and positive energy and is not fixated with preconceived ideas. That is the way that we move toward bettering ourselves, and that is the way we move toward true happiness in life.

If you are going right at the very root-consciousness level, then happiness and bliss are sure to be yours. Right consciousness means attentiveness, adaptability, and the ability to deal with the reality of every moment as it happens without following set patterns. This imbues great strength and delight within us because we respond properly to every situation.

Wrong consciousness always works according to its rigid patterns and is, therefore, unable to face the current realities. Hence, cultivate the right consciousness in every aspect of your life. With the correct foundation, you can catalyze all your various potentialities and abilities in life and move toward greater happiness and fulfillment in every way.

Right consciousness creates the dynamism of the spirit. It makes the right attitude in you. And that is what is truly needed in life. New solutions cannot come out of our old responses to old problems. We must be fresh in our consciousness. Freshness of consciousness is right consciousness. Freshness implies feeling rejuvenated, energized, delightful, and blissful.

CHAPTER 14

Finding Joy in Simple Things

Zen Buddhism is all about finding joy in the simplest and most minor tasks. The attitude of Zen is that if we enjoy small things and pour our good energy into small things, we can create true happiness for ourselves. Then, we can do larger things with the same spirit. It is the attitude with which you approach things! Nothing is too small or too big.

In Jainism, we can also see this attitude. Mahavir, the great Tirthankara of Jainism, exemplified it. He was concerned for the tiniest creatures, the smallest blade of grass even. He used to tell people not to harm anything. That is the whole great principle of *Ahimsa* or non-violence in Indian philosophy, something which Gandhi and many others emulated with great success in life also. In the West, Martin Luther King emulated this idea for the civil rights movement, realizing millions of dreams! In India, Dr BR Ambedkar is the ideal example of such principles.

The whole idea is that one looks upon the smallest things as important. That is real Ahimsa. It implies a concern for things, whether big or small, and is in no way antagonistic to those things. This is a core principle of Buddhism. It implies keeping an eye on non-antagonism toward small things. And when you can do that, you can look at the smallest phenomenon with love, compassion, dedication, and grace.

Mahatma Gandhi in India used to tell people that even if they are doing menial tasks they must do them with dedication! Many people used to get surprised when they went to his ashram because he used to make them do the so-called menial tasks. He used to make them do things they considered beneath them—cleaning the premises, taking care of others, paying heed to the lavatories, helping with their upkeep, and so on.

Eventually, the idea is to move away from egoistic attitudes and into a non-egoistic attitude of valuing the small things in life. If you can value the small things in life, you can be sure that you will move toward a more conscientious way of working and relating to others.

It is said that great people, when studied, show a very interesting trend in their childhood. Compared to others, they were more conscientious in their childhood chores, whether helping out in the kitchen, in the garden, with housework, cleaning their room, or making their bed. People who pay heed to small things always turn out to be more successful in life.

And this is a rule that applies to all things. It reflects the vision of the Buddhas as well as luminaries of various paths in Indian civilization for thousands of years.

CHAPTER 15

The Universe, Aliens & AI

Gautam Buddha was once asked how many living worlds exist in the universe. He said that there are more living worlds than grains of sand on earth!

Buddha's answer was mind-blowing. He was hinting at civilizations scattered around the universe, with conscious beings everywhere.

There is another story in Buddhism that says that once, Gautam Buddha's favorite disciple, Ananda, witnessed strange beings coming in the middle of the night to seek the audience of the Buddha. And Buddha seemed to have answered their questions. After they left, Ananda asked Gautam Buddha: "Bhante, who were these strange beings?" He said:

"On a distant galaxy, there is another Buddha, and his disciples saw the light coming from our world. They were curious about it, and they went and asked their Buddha permission to come here and question me." Ananda was awestruck!

So, the first thing is this curiosity, this expansion of our being to understand that consciousness is the fabric of the universe. It is the heartbeat of existence itself. Once we know this, our whole vista of life, happiness, etc., completely changes. We realize that we are fortunate to have taken birth upon this magnificent universe, full of consciousness. We value ourselves more. We are more grateful. Through that, we attain a higher blissfulness.

The other thing about consciousness is the idea of AI, artificial intelligence, or artificial consciousness. We can see that, as AI is moving ahead, consciousness can be born and generated repeatedly, even through mechanisms that we thought were impossible. It is not just human beings but creations that can attain consciousness. So, imagine that consciousness must be so prevalent within the very fabric of the universe. Knowing this, one can unlock one's mind and realize gratitude for life itself.

Gautam Buddha used to say that human beings are fortunate because we are on a plane of existence where material life is not all about happiness (unlike the higher planes of the devas or gods). Hence, we are curious about the question of sorrow and happiness, and neither are we in a hopeless situation like those who dwell in the lower worlds. Knowing all this, we must take the lesson of gratitude and realize that we are immensely free to expand ourselves to search.

The whole thing is about curiosity. It is about opening our beings to the understanding that we can guide ourselves toward a higher flowering of our own consciousness. Then, we participate in the eternal dance, which is the cosmos. That itself is a feeling of delight and joy. It is the greatest bliss!

CHAPTER 16

The Blissful Energy of Buddhist Statues

Have you ever thought about why the statues of the Buddha have such great appeal around the world?

Think about this: usually, you would not find people putting icons of a particular religion different from theirs within their living rooms. But you would see Buddha statues in living rooms worldwide, no matter what the homeowner's religion is! Buddha stands for the universal idea of spirituality, moving toward spiritual bliss. He symbolizes the universal state of being, which is an aspiration toward blissfulness.

The state of being represents the totality of noble and happy energy within you. And that is what we must emulate from the Buddha—this idea of being inwardly whole, this idea of creating such a beauty of energy within ourselves that we become unbreakable in the face of anything that we confront! It could be a life-and-death situation, a pandemic, a natural calamity—that does not matter.

What matters is the creation of harmonious energy within yourself, which creates bliss, delight, and joy. It makes your spiritual reality surface more and more.

You see, our material reality keeps changing. Yet, our spiritual reality is genuinely what we must aspire to, to not only make the heart and mind peaceful and happy but also strong enough to tap into our infinite, innate sources of energy. Endless sources of energy are available to us if we have the spiritual eye. We are children of the cosmos, of the wondrous universe.

We are all children of a vast reality! Let us tap into this vast reality and its subtle energy of joy. That is the whole art of Buddhism. It is the road to enlightenment! Yet, all this happens only by understanding that within you is an incredible treasure trove of spiritual ability.

Buddha statues are just a reminder of our spiritual ability within. Believe in that! You see, Buddhism requires no other belief. All that is needed is the belief that "yes, I too can be as the Buddha was!" The Buddha used to say that the only difference between him and the others is that he knows he is a Buddha, and others do not know that they are Buddhas. In other words, he is telling us to put the wholeness of our heart and mind and be into understanding our higher nature of blissfulness.

Once that is understood, you spontaneously move toward greater strength, greater self-empowerment, and greater centering within your higher possibilities. That is the very key to bliss and happiness. It allows you to maintain your individual strength and blissfulness through all the troubles that you may be going through . . . past all the doubts that may surface . . ., and through all the crises that may come your way.

CHAPTER 17

The Simplicity of a Happy Attitude

Bringing the simplicity of a happy attitude at work makes one more rooted in reality. This is key to the Buddha's teachings.

It is through simple, peaceful happiness that one removes the lens of ego. A happy vibe at work creates a more earthed, warm, down-to-earth insight into things.

Such insight always translates into non-egoistic clarity of heart and mind.

A person who works with a simple attitude will always be more productive and capable of abundance. Not only that, but he or she will spontaneously become a better leader in their workplace. The best way to express one's inner strength is to always have a blissful demeanor. There is no need to show other people at work a long face or a demeanor of constant dissatisfaction: somewhere, that only tells the other person that there is something dissatisfied within you, that you are not as successful as you should be at work.

A blissful person gives off the vibe of success. That is why creating an aura of bliss around you is very important. That way, not only do you become more charismatic, but other people are more able to respect you; subconsciously, we feel that a blissful person is a fulfilled person, a truly successful person. The creation of this vibe at your workplace allows you to become a person who is regarded as more capable, not less capable; a person who is more creative, not less creative; a person who is more successful, not less successful.

The old paradigm of success used to be a severe demeanor. In the world of today, in the rapidly flat and globalized planet that we live in, the new paradigm requires a new perspective that is one of carrying the vigor and delight of happiness wherever you go: through all your work relationships, networking, and so on. This makes you to be wanted, this makes you popular, but at the same time, it gives you an inner bounce of energy. And that is the most important thing to bring to earth. It creates *Purnata*, or wholeness of being, allowing you to be a better all-around achiever.

CHAPTER 18

Communicating Blissfulness

It is one thing to be personally happy. But it is as essential to communicate blissfulness to others. This is very important when it comes to Buddhism.

Buddhism is a religion that has always had monks spreading its word and teachings. But they had to do it in a manner that communicated happiness, joy, and well-being to others. Hence, Buddhism is efficient when it comes to interpersonal communication: within it, we see how they apply the principle of *Ananda*, bliss, or joy.

Communication is key when it comes to working and functioning efficiently in the world. The world of work is based on good communication: whether one is in marketing, pitching a product or service, or maintaining networks, it's all about excellence in communication. The best way to communicate with people is through a message of personal blissfulness, happiness, or joy. And that is what great brands in the world have always done. You can look at Coca-Cola: one important brand slogan of theirs is "Little drops of joy!"

Similarly, other brands sell this concept of delight and joy. Yet, the real idea of joyful communication is to feel yourself so full of passion and bliss within that you can share it with others. That makes it natural, and that keeps it spontaneous. That is why it is said that the best sales and marketing people are those who themselves bubbling with inner integrity and who believe in their product or service. That allows them to communicate truthfully with others.

People then buy into one's proposition as a natural and spontaneous happening.

Therefore, the inward integrity of your happiness is the most important. That way, one does not have to act, and one does not have to lie when one has the power of conviction within. Yes, in the past, people could get away with lying. But now, as we move toward the world where all the information is available at our fingertips, there is no point in lying.

Consumers can see the power of truth within communications. That is the best way because not only is the material aim realized, but also the spiritual aim- that one is doing a greater service to people by giving them something of joy. This is a key fundamental to finding the practical application of joyfulness within our workspaces. It leads to great spontaneity, joy, and energy. Communicate happily, blissfully!

Optimistic and non-selfish happiness is said to be an integral part of our consciousness. We must practice it through right thought, meditativeness, and sharing joy with others. This is the very fundamental teaching of all Indian spiritual paths. You can look at Sikhism, Buddhism, Hinduism,

Jainism, various mystical things of all masters and many paths in India emphasize the same thing.

They emphasize the importance and fundamental seed nature of happiness within our very spirit, our hearts, and our innate consciousness. Yet, how we allow that seed of happiness to grow into a tree, to give fruit and flower in our lives- and to *communicate it*- is all up to us.

A lot of people do not nurture the seed of happiness within themselves. And when you do not nurture the seed of happiness within you, you cannot expect it to create results for you. The remembrance of this fact leads you to a spontaneous affirmation of happiness within the work you communicate to the world. When you affirm yourself, happiness grows within you, and you can share it accordingly.

Through the fruit of your own bliss, you attain more seeds of happiness, which can be scattered into the world. Be like a person who is scattering seeds of happiness into the world. Make that your credo. A person who nurtures his or her own seeds of happiness can also spread these into the world. And then, one's life becomes fulfilled at all levels: at the level of work and the material, at the level of feelings and mind, and, at the level of the spiritual or mystical.

A person of true value can spread the seeds of joyfulness through work, relationships, consciousness, thoughts, and all one's communications and interactions with the world.

CHAPTER 19

Being In Tune
Within Yourself!

The Buddha used the example of a stringed instrument (the old Indian instrument called the *Veena*) as an ideal metaphor for the state of being that a human being needs to be in.

His idea was this: if the strings of the instrument are too tight, they will snap, and no music can be made from the instrument. If, on the other hand, the strings of the instrument are too loose, then, too, no music can be played. The instrument has to be put into tune, not put under too much pressure by over-tightening, or too lackadaisical and lazy, too loose or non-alert. And this is an apt parallel with man's state of being.

Often, we put ourselves under too much pressure—in our work, relationships, etc.—and, therefore, cannot function with the totality of our energy and intelligence. And this only leads to sorrow. On the other hand, we often become very lax in our attitude and too laid back. And that, too, is not good for us. The idea is to balance a high state of energy with the softness and sensitivity of being. Then only do we come into tune with ourselves. Do not be too hard on yourself, and do not be too soft in your approach to life. Both qualities are needed.

It is often thought that in today's 'dog eat dog' world, we need to be very hard. But remember that the blade of grass survives the storm; it does not break, and the great significant tree snaps. It is because of the blade of grass's pliability and flexibility, softness that it is able to withstand the challenge. So, too, we must be. Both strength and softness are needed in life. That brings about natural and spontaneous happiness or bliss.

CHAPTER 20

The *Sahaj* Path

Buddhism has often been called the *Sahaj* or simple path. It requires us to become more and more grounded within our natural being. In other words, the way of spontaneity and simplicity, by being completely grounded in oneself, is the way of the Buddha. What this does is nourish your inner strength and energy.

We live in a world of so many distractions: we have the mobile phone, so much entertainment, and so many things we feel we need to attend to. So somewhere, we forget being established more and more within ourselves. The whole art of Buddhist meditation is to go back deeper and deeper into the self, to dive deep into the inner recesses of the mind and one's inner energies. That is what the whole spiritual science of *chakras* means: to go into one's innate energies.

It is said that the guru also exists within us. So does the power of existence itself. Hence, when we ground ourselves in our being, we realize that there is something within us that is of the beyond. The body and mind are not as important as we think. That way, the depths of your being become filled with a natural and spontaneous joy because now you are on the path of self-realization. Self-realization is the greatest bliss and the greatest happiness in life.

CHAPTER 21

The Warrior's Self-belief

Buddha teaches us to have self-belief. Self-belief means that even amid your darkest moments, in the so-called dark night of the soul, when you are facing difficult circumstances, somewhere, you have the optimism that after every night comes a new dawn. In other words, you are never to feel hopeless. An optimistic attitude is the root of self-belief. It means the ability to not look at it from the point of success or failure about whether you will come out victorious or not. But it is your attitude that no matter what, you will fight the fight, and as a good warrior, you should fight the battle!

The best warrior is one who is concerned with his attitude toward warriors. It is *how* you fight the fight! The result may come as destined, or the result may be based on certain outside factors outside your control. You cannot control everything! What you can control is your ability to have an attitude of self-belief. That itself creates hope. And through hope, you attain greater happiness. Then, you are not afraid of what is to come tomorrow. You become fearless and courageous. And courage, ultimately, is the biggest catalyst to creating happiness in our lives. Without courage, there can never be true happiness. Without courage, there can never be any true dynamism in our lives.

Yes, it is not good to be foolhardy, have too much hope, or be overoptimistic. You must be balanced in your approach. You must be ready even for defeat. But you must not have a defeatist attitude. Self-belief means having a victorious attitude. Victory begins in the spiritual heart of the warrior. That is the true attitude of the warrior.

CHAPTER 22

The Question of Artificial Intelligence vs. Soulfulness

Today is the age of artificial intelligence. We have seen massive quantum leaps in computing. And most certainly, very soon, artificial intelligence will be far more capable of performing tasks that we cannot even imagine. Yet can artificial intelligence bring the quality of soulfulness and heartfulness to what we do?

Soulfulness and heartfulness mean bringing the core of our spiritual strength into our work, into our activities, and bringing our wholeness of mind, body, and spirit energies into whatever it is we do. It means going beyond logic, beyond artificially created intelligence, beyond thought constructs and systems. In other words, we are to go beyond the psychological, the physiological, etc., and maximize our work happiness, our quality of playfulness, our heartfulness, and our soulfulness in whatever we do.

In Indian traditions, this has been called the quality of playfulness, where you creatively and happily bring in whatever qualities of your heart and soul into all your activities. And this has become the new paradigm of today's companies. For example, today's Google, Apple, or LinkedIn encourage their employees to have a sense of fun at work and creativity at work. Only then can they do something meaningful, something that leads to value-creation for all.

It is about happiness or *Ananda* as the basic philosophy of happiness for the employees, as well as for the customers, because when employees are happy, they automatically create work that is beneficial for the customers. That is why these companies, including Google and LinkedIn, encourage celebration at work. Often, you would see their employees' celebrating occasions like Halloween, etc.

It is all about the fact that in the superfast work environment, we also have to bring our greatest qualities of heart and go beyond logic. That is the very crux of Buddhism.

CHAPTER 23

Focus vs. Awareness

It is good to be focused on practical things for example, if one is accomplishing a task or taking an exam. However, from the Buddha's point of view, *awareness is more important than focus.*

Focus means you limit the mind, and you narrow it down to a particular task. Awareness means that you expand yourself. The Buddha's way is all about expansion, expanding one's energy so that all the dimensions and energies of one is being start functioning to their most sensitive and powerful degree.

In the state of focus, we are never relaxed. In the state of awareness, we are relaxed even amidst the hardest task. So, in Zen Buddhism, the expert archer or the expert swordsman functions through this expanded awareness and focus on archery or sword fighting comes as a by-product of that awareness.

All human breakthroughs come about through greater awareness, which is why not everybody can produce innovative breakthroughs like Einstein can. An Einstein defocuses the mind from what is known and expands the mind through greater awareness of the unknown. And through that unknown dimension comes all the success, bliss, relaxedness, and an unstrained or effortless effort.

Creativity, in particular, requires awareness more than focus because you have to think outside the box, whereas focus sometimes keeps us concentrated within the box. Hence, focus more on expanding your awareness than just on narrow goals. That is the way to true happiness in life.

CHAPTER 24

Inner Power

The Buddha's way was to awaken the inner power of our being. True inner power comes from having strength, compassion and empathy. In other words, be as gentle as a blade of grass, yet have the resilience of a great tree and have the sensitivity to perceive the world and perceive all of existence more sensitively.

That way that self-potential within you of Buddhahood arises and creates a spontaneous bliss.

We are to exist in a state of being where we do not harden ourselves and become insensitive. We must be extremely sensitive to our environment, and we must have a sense of awe and wonder about this beautiful existence. Yet, simultaneously, we should not be so weak in spirit that the slightest thing disturbs us emotionally, to break us.

Most people, no matter how strong they seem inwardly, get broken when faced with difficult situations in life. The true Buddhist does not get broken by crisis at all. Rather, the true Buddhist is a beacon for others: a pillar of reliability who has the capacity to absorb the shocks that life throws.

This capacity for absorption is the key to the Buddha's message. It awakens inner power. The Buddha himself demonstrated this many times in his life. Notably, once, when somebody came and spat on him, Buddha did not react. And the people around him were surprised. Buddha remained completely calm! By doing so, he conveyed and demonstrated this wordless silent teaching to his *Sangha* or congregation: that even one who has such great power as the living Buddha does not resort to using that power negatively or in a reactionary way when faced with any sort of antagonistic or unfavorable situation. That is the real strength of the Buddhas, the secret of their bliss, and it should be ours, too!

By absorbing the insult of the person who sought to disgrace him, Buddha showed that the true Buddhist is not disturbed through emotional turmoil but is firmly established in their nature of Buddha-bliss.

CHAPTER 25

The Whole Cosmos Has Consciousness!

Buddhism has consistently held that not just humans have self-awareness and consciousness. Our whole cosmos is teaming with beings who are self-aware and have consciousness.

We can see it in our animal world. It used to be thought that animals are not self-aware. However, increasingly, through studies in neuroscience on animals, we have found that animals are exceedingly self-aware. Of course, the more intelligent animals, such as elephants, are known to be such—and elephants have a very special place in Buddhism! But even ants have been demonstrated to have self-awareness.

So, beings share this common intelligence, this pool of intelligence. Intelligence is teaming within the universe. Yet, because human beings have complicated their lives and confined their minds to conditioned patterns and conditioned thoughts or institutionalized thoughts, they cannot understand the meaning of free thoughts. Buddhism is about our original and independent or natural self-awareness and consciousness. That is the whole quest of meditation: to bring us back to our natural self-awareness and consciousness. In other words, our highest capabilities are obscured, like clouds obscure the sky and the sun. But behind it, the sky is illuminated by the sun.

So, do not let your ideas of conditioned patterns stop your freedom of mind and heart. The Bodhisattvas' previous incarnations have been animal forms in Buddhism, especially the Jataka Tales. But at each birth, that being has strived toward greater self-awareness and higher consciousness. And that should be the whole quest of every human being.

Our desire to move toward greater self-awareness and higher consciousness triggers a flow of bliss within all our activities. It evolves us, lifts us higher, makes us take the quantum leap out of all patterned structures, and makes us completely free to find our own bliss.

CHAPTER 26

Jiddu Krishnamurti and The Buddha

The great mystic and spiritual philosopher Jiddu Krishnamurti was once asked what his secret was. And J. Krishnamurti just said, "My only secret is that I don't mind." In other words, Krishnamurti implies that no matter what happens in life, nothing should damage you so much that you start feeling bad or *minding* things.

Always remember that just as the waves come and go upon the ocean, yet the ocean remains calm, deep, and beautifully silent within its depths, so too, we must be. Do not get identified by the waves which keep changing. Identify yourself with your inner depths, that ocean of happiness, that oceanic bliss that exists within you. There is a great reservoir of bliss within you. Let nothing disturb that!

And J. Krishnamurti himself was trained in very deep, in fact, the deepest Buddhist methods. He used to say that everything is contained within the Buddhist texts, even though he never liked to emphasize a particular religion or religious path. Cosmic bliss is indeed a mighty ocean. How we let it function within our lives is always a choice. The potential for happiness is in every drop of water flowing within this ocean dynamically, in every moment of our lives.

Do not make happiness dependent on a particular successful event at work, and so on. That is the usual tendency of man. Rather, make happiness part of your own flow. This concept of flow is very prevalent in today's neuroscience and popular psychology. Be in a state of flow. Remember that your oceanic bliss within is always available for you to tap into, to draw from, and to strengthen yourself with its healing waters.

The concept of flow or spontaneous intuitive actualization of self-potential at work, especially, has, in fact, become a vital part of assessing work quality these days. It is the new paradigm of well-being and happiness at work and is a standing testament to what the ancient wisdom of Buddhism always talked about.

In India, of course, it is said that the river Ganges purifies us. The relationship between rivers and mankind is very deep and metaphorical in India. The waters of the rivers cleans us. The Ganges is a metaphor for *Aranda*, for ultimate bliss. By remembering this principle of letting the bliss flow within you, no matter what happens on the exterior, you are emphasizing the dynamic undercurrent of well-being and happiness that is always accessible by you, provided you begin thinking of it that way!

And in India, not only can we see the rivers and oceans important but there is a metaphor for the river Saraswati, which is supposed to be the hidden river flowing within an underground river- it cannot be seen as the Ganges or the Yamuna. Yet, it is named after the goddess of learning.

So, true learning is to remember that knowledge of blissfulness that exists within you, that Saraswati that resides within you, flowing deep within you. The remembrance of this very fact fills you with greater and greater happiness and joy.

CHAPTER 27

Physical Well-being

The Buddha emphasized spiritual, mental and physical well-being for happiness and bliss.

Usually, we do not associate the Buddha with physical exertion. However, in Buddhist practice, there are numerous techniques for relaxing the physical aspect of ourselves through discipline. These could be various Yogas and techniques, breathing exercises, and so on.

The ultimate aim of all yoga, whether in the Buddhist or Hindu context, is to achieve such a relaxation of our being that we can more easily move into the meditative state. You see, Buddhism is very rich in physical culture. For example, the great Zen master from South India, Bodhidharma, began the martial disciplines in the Shaolin Temple of China. From that, the whole idea of Kung fu in China, Taekwondo in South Korea, Judo, Karate, and Aikido in Japan took birth.

Treat and look after yourself physically, and then you will be more able to explore the deeper aspects of the Buddha's message, which is *Jhāna* (or Dhyana in Sanskrit, meditation).

Eventually, to achieve true bliss and happiness, we must strive toward physical, mental, and spiritual relaxation and wellness.

CHAPTER 28

Moving toward Silence

Look at a painting or a statue of the Buddha: does it look like he is disturbed or shaken by anything? No! The state of Buddhahood is one of unshakable inner non-disturbance and utter inner silence. And in that inner silence, one attains a great power center within oneself. No matter what happens on the outside, one's energy within is unshaken. That is how the Buddha-nature is!

On the outside, everything can come and go. There can be so many distractions. Yet, at the very center of your being, you should be unshaken by anything. We get shaken and disturbed because the mind is reactive. Yet the unshaken state is one where there is no mind! One's mind has merged into the universal mind. There is no sense of individual time. There is no sense of the individual getting perturbed by any particular happening.

Remaining unshaken is the root of true bliss in life. All outer events happen in the material sphere. The sphere of the mystical or material is one where you are completely non-distracted by thoughts, you are completely non-distracted by memories, desires, and so on. And that leads to real peace. And where there is real peace, there is real happiness and bliss.

CHAPTER 29

Strengthening Yourself

Buddhism teaches us to strengthen ourselves, not only at the level of mind and body but also at the level of spirit. When it comes to the body, you must remember that while Buddhism on the one hand emphasizes calm meditation, it is also the progenitor of martial arts.

Both meditation and martial arts are born of Buddhism. And martial arts were invented as exercises for the body to withstand the rigors of meditation.

We must emphasize and not neglect our body and keep it in shape, because keeping the body in a pure state of being, in a vigorous and lean state of being, automatically brings delight and joy within us. This strengthens us and makes us less vulnerable in the face of life's challenges, especially bodily and physical challenges.

Of course, the second thing is to strengthen thoughts and emotions. In other words, we are to make the consciousness such that it can function with utter confidence yet utter quietness. The quiet mind is regarded in Buddhism as the ideal mind, the joyful and blissful mind. The quiet mind or the listening mind is the one that is able to resist and encounter all sorts of situations without being agitated.

Non-agitation of our consciousness is the goal: it is the secret of happiness. The person who attains the sense of non-agitation goes beyond being disturbed by outer circumstances. And when you are not disturbed, you become far more capable of utilizing your energy in a positive manner to encounter the crisis or challenge in front of you.

Then, no challenge in life scares you, no matter if the challenge is a physical one, an existential one, or one that has to do with any other aspect of our life, such as relationships or work.

The whole idea of Buddhism is maximizing our inward ability for resilience. This leads to peace or Shaanti within us and a great power or Bala of being, which in turn leads to blissfulness.

CHAPTER 30

Learn to Ignore Thoughts

Sometimes, we have just to ignore our own thoughts. This is key to catalyzing Ananda's state of being. We should not let the mind's anxious thoughts override the spontaneous peacefulness and happiness we can feel.

You know, our thoughts keep finding different ways to put us down at work or in relationships. For example, when somebody insults us in a work situation or at work or castigates or reprimands us, we feel so bad that the other person is able to drain us of our energy, creativity, and happiness. Our inner abundance is lost, and we become prevented from being creators of abundance and happy people.

Always remember the principle which Buddha used to talk about. One day, somebody insulted him in his assembly, the *Sangha*. And people were surprised at how calmly Buddha reacted. He did not react, in fact! He simply remained smiling, calm, and tranquil. And once the person insulted him left, his disciples asked him, how come he was totally unruffled. Buddha had a very simple answer. He said: "The person tried to insult me, but it was up to me whether to take the insult. I chose not to take the insult."

So, this is a great lesson for happiness: Do not let your thoughts and reactivity take away your own happiness. Sometimes, we become our worst enemies when we do that. In this Buddha anecdote, the important thing to remember is that the person who had insulted him ultimately came back and apologized for his own actions, and in fact, became a follower of the Buddha!

So, a non-reactive person who does not pay too much heed to the negative thoughts triggered by somebody's bad behavior, and will always be more powerful and happy, whether at work or in relationships. This is a great affirmation of the Indian wisdom of Ananda, or blissfulness.

CHAPTER 31

The Principle of Emptiness

The principle of emptiness is very important in Buddhism. The Buddha encourages us to cultivate a state of mental emptiness, free of conditioning.

When the mind is empty, it flows in whatever direction it needs to be channeled toward. The empty mind implies the one that is not bound by any preconceived ideas or notions. It is the mind that is able to go past all the rigidity of ideologies, dogmas, emotions, and conditionings. Emptiness in Buddhism implies complete openness, not getting tied down by any particular concept. This allows us to be very light.

The idea of *Laghima, or lightness of mind,* is key to understanding how we can move toward happiness. A heavy mind and a heavy heart are those that are bound down by the constant flux of changing circumstances and our reactions to them. Heaviness implies the emotionally heavy mind, which is structured by its moods. The empty mind means the unstructured mind. It is the original mind.

In Zen Buddhism, it is called "the beginner's mind" or the fresh mind, which is able to forget the thoughts of yesterday and flow on dynamically within the present moment. In other words, the empty mind implies that which can go past all blockages without any self-consciousness. It is the easy and balanced approach to remaining mentally happy.

CHAPTER 32

Be Detached from Hurt

From the Buddha's point of view, one of the biggest impediments to happiness and bliss is that we remain too attached to past sufferings, insults, or hurt. Most human beings cannot get over something bad that has happened in the past: a bad feeling lingers, and they continue to be affected by something somebody did or said to them in the past. That completely stops our evolution toward *Ananda* or Bliss.

From the Buddhist point of view, the ability to withstand hurt and insult is very important. In fact, which is the very hallmark of a true Buddhist or anybody who wishes to follow the Buddha. A little hurt will not really kill you. Yet, a little hurt can become damaging if you cling to it if you do not let go of it. Whatever happened in the past, let It go, do not create a bigger issue out of how somebody insulted you, tried to break your spirit, and so on. That will only create more damage in the long term.

Deal with your hurt. You got hurt; you can cry over it but then leave it behind. The biggest problem is *clinginess*. And this idea of being detached from one's feelings of hurtfulness is the true way to emerge into this blissful state. Once you let go, you become filled with joy, and like a flower, you bloom with all your happiness, sending your fragrance out into the world. When you do that, people are automatically affected, in a good way, by your state of inner bliss. And as bees come to a flower, they become attracted to your very being, your very vibe.

CHAPTER 33

Being Grounded
in Happiness

The Buddha used to say, "I teach because you and all beings want to have happiness and want to avoid suffering. I teach the way things are." Buddha's emphasis is on helping us move toward and be grounded in happiness and bliss. Even during today's tough times, his teachings are the most relevant for the subject of happiness because he gives us the gift of insight or *Pragya*, which is a spiritual attitude toward life.

When we are grounded in this spiritual attitude, we become automatically more well-equipped to create bliss for ourselves and others. That way, we will also be respected. Gautam Buddha says: "He who is full of faith and virtue in whatever land he travels is respected everywhere!" So, a fundamental teaching on his path to happiness is to become full of faith and virtue, and then automatically, respect is born. It is all about awakening our inner consciousness—the state of *Bodhi*. Then, no matter what you do in life, you become inclined to bliss.

Buddha says, "Bliss is attainable by everyone who walks on the noble path." This is his biggest assurance that if we inculcate higher consciousness within our beings, we attain bliss of all kinds, and with it, clarity, brilliance, intuitive ability, etc.

We must create dignity within our consciousness, a nobility of heart called Arya in Pali. This aligns us to have joyful enthusiasm and energy within ourselves. When we have joyful energy and enthusiasm within ourselves, we automatically create the root-level strength to fructify our life's work and vision into flowering and fruition.

At the heart of Buddha's message is the message of excellence cultivated through a dynamic blissfulness within us. It is the greatest force within you. We just have to unlock the great fount of bliss within.

CHAPTER 34

Psychology

The great French psychologist Emile Coué has given a lovely mantra for bettering oneself. It is a positive affirmation reminder to oneself, and it goes like this: "Every day, in every way, I will be better and better." Emile Coué has come very close to understanding the very heart of the Buddha's message because the Buddha always wanted us to keep improving ourselves.

In the Buddha's view, there is no limits to the virtues and the betterment we can acquire. Certain limitations bind all things within the material world. However, human beings are not bound by any limitations within the domain of the internal. Within you, you are infinite. Remembering this, you feel great freedom and great happiness arising within you, great freedom and happiness arising within you because suddenly realize that the limitations that you think you have simply been placed by you yourself.

In your internal being, there is absolutely no limit. The only limiting factor in life is the ego. By removing our ego, we lose all boundaries between ourselves and universal energy. We merge into universal energy itself, and that brings us great joy, delight, happiness, and blissfulness.

CHAPTER 35

Withstanding Pain

Your ability to withstand hurt or pain (physical, emotional, or mental) is the path to true happiness. The Buddha taught about inner energy and inner peace. Both inner energy and inner peace come about when you are able to very patiently withstand any kind of hurt. That is true maturity. That is the way of the true practitioner of the Buddha's path because then, their totality of energy is not disturbed.

Usually, our energy gets disturbed by some hurt that we feel, in whatever form, be it through a personal relationship, a work-related issue, or something else. For your energy to truly flow with its greatest strength, you must understand that no matter what, you are able to very patiently remain undisturbed and undistracted by all that you perceive to be painful in your life. That is the strength that the Buddhas themselves personify.

Look at a statue of a Buddha. He seems completely undisturbed, completely at peace, and completely strong . . . infinitely strong. Make your being more and more like that, and nothing can affect you. You establish yourself in an inner state of bliss and peace, which can never be taken away from you.

CHAPTER 36

The Inquisitive Mind

The mind of the true Buddhist is inquisitive—that is, it is searching and always inquisitive about truth.

Such inquisitiveness is considered the very basis of all true fulfillment in life. When we are inquisitive about our larger existence: why we exist and how we should best live our lives, that creates great energy. As the great Jesus says, it is, "knock, and the door shall be open; seek, and you shall find." This seeking, this basic curiosity after the ultimate questions in life, is at the very heart of Buddha's message. It generates its delight, its joy, its spontaneous bliss and happiness.

Without inquisitiveness, there is no real joy. Usually, religions have ready-made answers. They tell us to believe in something or the other. But in Buddhism, the beauty is that *one does not really need to believe in anything as such.* The only thing one really needs to do is to inquire and be inquisitive about the truth. Then, all the answers come to oneself very naturally. That is why Buddhism is considered the most philosophical of all the religious and mystical paths.

At the base of this idea, which is also reflected in Hinduism as the state of Mumukshu, striving after truth and having a thirst for truth. And in fact, before he became the Buddha, Siddhartha Gautam was all about striving and being inquisitive about the ultimate truth in life. That is how he attained the true bliss of the Buddhas.

Nothing Can Confine Truth!

The Buddha taught that no institution or organization can confine truth.

All the ideals and ideas that exist within the boundaries of institutions and conditioned patterns ultimately do not point the way to unhindered, ultimate truth. Therefore, they cannot bring about true and infinite bliss within the hearts and minds of human beings. We must learn to see outside the boundaries of ideologies or institutions.

Human beings are experts at creating institutions and organizations. We are experts at segregating truths, considering ourselves separate from others. But ultimately, we are part of the same universal existence. And if we bind ourselves within a confined pattern, we can never find that unending, blissful feeling in the fabric of existence itself.

Always remember the golden rule: doubt the veracity of institutions and organizations. That is the greatest act in life. Yet very few people have the guts to look beyond what they are conditioned to look at. The true seeker on the path of the Buddha is willing to sacrifice the limitations of institutions and, thereby, move toward ultimate bliss.

The whole idea and the light of the Buddhas point toward freeing the mind. The act of freeing the mind automatically leads to spontaneous delight and joy. Your true potential as a human being becomes truly awakened and unlocked when you go beyond the limited truth of the known and enter into the field of the unknown. The Buddhas exist within the infinite dimensions of the unknown, always expanding toward cosmic beings.

CHAPTER 38

Materialism

Do not base your happiness upon material outcomes. Material outcomes are often a matter of chance in various circumstances. Always base your being upon your inner blissfulness, your inner Buddha state. Make your inner being vibrate with peace, energy, a sense of freedom, and a sense that life and death are but parts of one integrated and wonderful reality.

By discovering the deathless spiritual part of ourselves, we can transcend all worries and troubles and move effortlessly toward self-happiness. That is the promise of the Buddhas, their idea of the meditative state.

Buddhism is not so much about the act of prayer as it is about the attitude of meditativeness. The difference between prayer and meditation is actually not much. Yet, it is subtle. Prayer emphasizes reverence for an unknown force. Meditation emphasizes the discovery of one's essential unity with a higher source. And that makes one blissful!

Buddha's way is of meditation, of understanding our link with the higher. Yet, implied within this is a natural prayerfulness: a prayerfulness that does not take 'God' to be a higher being to be feared. It does not even need a deity as such because it believes in establishing ourselves within the blissfulness of Infinity.

The power of the Infinite can be given many names: ultimate reality, God, the absolute, and so on. That does not really matter in the end. What really matters is living the message of that infinite power through your mind-body-spirit; when you do that, you automatically become blissful and happy.

CHAPTER 39

Tranquility: The Way of the Mystic Warrior

Tranquility is the Buddhist key to happiness. It means having a soothing and serene inner quality, an energy of relaxation, inward rest, and inward quietness. A person who has these qualities can be inwardly happy.

There is no bliss possible without tranquility. Hence, remember to be inwardly tranquil in all your work and relationship situations. It implies not being ruffled by things, never losing your bearings through anger, anxiety, and so on!

In all things, be alert to the higher wisdom of remaining balanced or *Santulit*, and have equipoise within your being. This is also the lesson of the great scripture, the Bhagvad Gita in which Lord Krishna advises Prince Arjuna to be completely calm, serene, and tranquil, even amid such dangerous work as that of a warrior on the battlefield. And following Krishna's advice, Arjuna can become a better warrior.

Hence, the way of true *Ananda*, happiness, or bliss is the way of the mystic warrior: a person who, even when faced with danger, can carry a certain bliss within their hearts and minds and thereby become even more intense, passionate, and effective in all that they attempt.

CHAPTER 40

You Do Not Have to Become Anything!

We are constantly trying to become something, to attain name, fame, power, position, etc. That is the way of the world. But the Buddha's view is very revolutionary: He teaches that we do not have to become anybody; we just have to be established in our own state of being, our own 'suchness'.

In fact, one of the very famous words for the Buddha is the '*Tathagata*', the one who is completely established in his *suchness*.

Establishing yourself within your being, not constantly trying to be somebody based on your thoughts and ambitions, is the way to attain silence within your being. It creates great peace and soulful energy within you. You become a witness to all things. You become highly aware and awakened to your inner energy. So, you suddenly find that there is no need to become somebody. You are already infinitely powerful within yourself.

This idea of suchness leads to self-potential realization. It unlocks us from the need to become and, instead, to be more of what we already are. Essentially, the goal of Buddhism is self-realization. Self-realization always begins with being established in your suchness. That is the true path to bliss and fulfillment in life.

CHAPTER 41

Have the Quality of the Lotus

The ideal of Buddhist thought regarding the state of Ananda, or supreme happiness, is the lotus flower. It is a key symbol of the various paths of spirituality.

The lotus, amidst the murky and sometimes dirty water it exists within, still does what it has to do: it blooms and blossoms to its uttermost beauty! It spreads its charm. In other words, it is undaunted by all that exists within. That should be our ideal for life if we want to attain a state of happiness. Be like the lotus!

There are all kinds of people around us. There are all sorts of circumstances which arise in one's life. Yet, remember this ideal of the lotus. Then, nothing can touch you. The world's trials and tribulations do not touch you when you have such an attitude. You are just to do what you have to do: blossom to the fullest ability of yourself, the fullest potential of yourself. And if you can do that, nothing can stop you from greater success and fulfillment. And, more importantly, from touching the highest peaks of inner joy of which you are capable! And that is true fulfillment in life.

The lotus is a reminder of our potential for mind-body-spirit wellness and bliss or *Ananda* amidst all odds!

CHAPTER 42

Aapo Deepo Bhava

The Buddha used to say: "*Aapo Deepo Bhava*"—light the lamp within your being!

Your inner light has great power to dispel all darkness within yourself. In other words, you have the means to enlighten yourself, to make yourself completely blissful, no matter what happens in the external world. Remembering this is at the very heart of understanding the Buddha's message.

The whole idea is that no matter what situation you are suffering from- relationship-related, work-related, etc.- the best way is to concentrate on illumining yourself through your own inner understanding and inner self-realization. That is the biggest antidote to all the problems in life because when you are filled with your inner light of consciousness, you automatically move toward solving all external problems.

Ultimately, how you are within your being determines your degree of blissfulness. Remembering this is to absorb the Buddha's message.

CHAPTER 43

Simplicity Creates Great Things

S implicity creates strength, purity, wisdom, happiness, and all good things. And the way of the Buddha is one of simplicity. The Buddha used to teach that it is only the simple person who is able to keep the mind in the present moment. When we become too complicated, we keep thinking about the past or the future.

Simplicity means being willing to go with the river of life as it flows. Yes, you are awake, aware, and alert. But you are also humble enough to recognize that anything may happen tomorrow, and through simplicity, you are willing to meet any challenges in life.

Simplicity is considered a divine quality in Buddhism, Hinduism, and indeed in all world spirituality. It cannot be really taught through religious books as such. It is simply a quality of the mind; it is a natural quality that needs to surface more and more within you. The Buddha's mind is a mind which is completely simple and clear.

Clarity is the main virtue that arises out of simplicity. Through clarity, we are able to connect to universal joy, delight, and bliss more and more. Simplicity is nothing to learn. It is rather to be established in your own natural being and through that, shine with your own self-luminous light.

CHAPTER 44

Being Choiceless

The Buddha's state is one of choiceless and effortless awareness. In other words, it is a quality of seeing clearly as things are instead of doing anything.

This state of being is attainable. We must remember that we are to become a witness to all things. Whatever happens, we remain effortless and choiceless perceptive of it. There is no need to really make an effort.

All you have to do is clear your mind and see things. Then, insight will automatically come to you. Energy will automatically arise in you. And that energy is joyful. Energy is delightful when it comes about as the result of clarity of perception.

So, the foundation of happiness is to remain choiceless. One does not have to choose all the time. The human mind is a constant chooser. The Buddha mind is one where all questions of choice have disappeared. Whatever comes is seen with clear eyes. Then, within your mind, you become silent, wise, and full of a dynamism that shows you, very transparently, your own ability to be completely blissful.

It creates a sort of detachment in you, where you can perceive things with purity and, thereby, act as needed within the moment.

This moment-to-moment effortless and choiceless awareness is the very key that we must imbibe and practice in our lives. It is the essence of Buddhism itself. It creates spontaneous bliss within you. It cleanses you of all your anxieties.

It makes your inner light shine brighter. And when that happens, you become illumined and happy in whatever you do.

CHAPTER 45

Evolution

Often, we think that our frustrations and anxieties hinder us and impede our evolution. But in reality, they can become the starting point for a new evolution within you.

In fact, Gautam Buddha himself experienced so much frustration and anxiety about human existence when he confronted the four sights when he was a prince (a man bent with old age, a person afflicted with sickness, a corpse, and a wandering ascetic).

It is all about your attitude that you take toward your particular frustration, which determines how much you will evolve. If you look at it as a starting point for the quantum leap of your soul, then it acts like a springboard and takes you to a higher level of existence than you have ever known.

It is very interesting because several religious texts of India begin with a person who is seemingly frustrated, anxious, and hopeless in life. We can see that in the Bhagvad Gita, where the warrior prince Arjun is in a state of complete despair and hopelessness, and the divine call of Krishna lifts him out of that morass of frustration.

Hence, never feel that your low points in life will continually be low and will keep you low. Remember that they are simply the start of a new, fresher journey toward greater blissfulness. With that in mind, you transform all your frustrations and anxieties into something productive.

CHAPTER 46

Finding True Purpose in Life

When we have true purpose in life, we automatically become happier and more joyful. The very root of finding purpose in life stems from the realization that you are an utterly unique individual. You stand for something that is an expression of the divine. You are a hidden Buddha! You are not here on earth for the ordinary. No!

There is something truly extraordinary to be created through your life and your work! Have this faith, have this understanding, because through it, you become blissful, and you are able to bring more meaning and purpose into whatever you do.

And then whatever work you do takes on great power, strength, vigor, zeal, and *Ananda*. Remember this always: the uniqueness of our being is a foundational teaching of Buddhism.

CHAPTER 47

Mind–Body–Spirit Balance

The idea of *Santulan* or mind-body-spirit balance is the aim of Buddhist practices. We must balance all aspects of our lives: our diet, our sex life, our work life, and so on. True well-being is attuning yourself to such a good state of balance that you feel spontaneous joy. Imbalance in any area of our life (physical, mental, emotional, and spiritual) creates unhappiness.

In the yogic traditions of Buddhism and Hinduism, it is important that we look after ourselves physically, begin with balance in our physical sphere, and then move on to mental and emotional balance. Then spontaneously, we become more equipped for the balanced state of bliss in the mystical or spiritual domain.

CHAPTER 48

The Power of Compassion

Compassion is very powerful - it creates inspiration. Compassion creates spiritual evolution and the highest bliss.

The idea of *Karuna*, or compassion, is central to the Buddha. His very energy flows in a state of compassion, and through that compassion, we feel blissful. Whenever we look at a statue of the Buddha, we can feel that vibe of his touching our soul. And that is the way we must also be.

Think about it: if you really want to move people, the positive energy of compassion is required. Then, not only does it fulfill you and make you happy, bringing about great joy in your being, but it also sparks joy in the other person's being. That is the secret of truly charismatic people, truly good people. Compassion makes a person more inspired, more creative, and more able to reach out with new good ideas that can be of value in the world.

The importance of this inner state of compassion lies at the deepest levels of Buddhism.

It is all about having good energy within oneself, and with the world. It is the true, real prayer. Compassion is the real *Sadhana* or spiritual practice in Buddhism. It energizes us and creates dynamism, apart from the highest bliss.

CHAPTER 49

The Buddha's Mystic Philosophy

The Buddha's mystic philosophy is a very practical one. It teaches us how to be at inner peace and happiness even amidst an ever-changing and dynamic world.

We live in a world where everything changes every day. Various epidemics, economic crashes, military conflicts, and so many other things disrupt our view of life. This dynamism or change is inherent in the very fabric of existence. It is part of life's flow. But we must never be bewildered by this change. We must maintain great equipoise and calmness within.

Buddha symbolizes this calmness, this inner peace, this state of inner bliss that is beyond all outer changes.

There is so much uncertainty in life. Nothing is truly permanent. And often, our mindset does not adjust to these changes. We become scared by how changes happen in the world. We become insecure about what will happen tomorrow. But the Buddha's way is about maintaining a fresh flow of consciousness within everything and every circumstance. This creates a continuous feeling of inner strength and blissfulness and resilience to all sorts of outward changes.

A true evolution of the human soul is when it can maintain its spiritual strength, no matter what happens outwardly. When, within our inner being, we maintain calmness, equipoise, and peace, we automatically move toward an abiding happiness that is unaffected by the outer.

CHAPTER 50

The Most
Valuable Lessons

The Buddha teaches us the most valuable lessons for happiness, especially when life looks tough and when facing challenges.

The Buddha's way is for all-round happiness in life: in our work, in our meditation, and in our relationships. True fulfillment is the very hallmark of the

Buddha's way of life. This is because the Buddha goes deeply into life's most essential questions and factors, which is why many people have been attracted to Buddhist philosophy over the years. A good example is Steve Jobs, who founded Apple Computer. Essentially, anything based on Buddhist principles creates happiness, just as the iPhone has created for millions of people worldwide.

Buddhism teaches us to be of great functional value in the world. And that is the essence of the lesson we can glean from its aesthetic. It tells us that we must move toward self-realization, self-belief, and an internalized state of being.

Within our internal selves, we are essentially fearless; we are essentially capable of great excellence. It is just our attitude within the world which allows these virtues to surface. In Buddhism, the true virtue is to create a good energy field within and around oneself through feelings of compassion and well-being for all. Hence, Buddhism teaches us value creation when it comes to work or play.

CHAPTER 51

Buddhism's 'Ten Perfections' for Enlightened Bliss

Buddhism teaches us the 'ten perfections' (*in classical Buddhism, it is called paramita;* in Tibetan Buddhism, it is called *pha rol tu phyin pa;* in Chinese Buddhism, it is called *du or boluomi*). If we strive toward these *ten perfections of being,*

we attain spontaneous bliss, great spiritual delight, elation, rapture, and joy.

These ten perfections are:
1. The perfection of giving, which is called *danaparamita*.
2. The perfection of morality, which is called *shilaparamita*.
3. The perfection of patience, which is called *kshantiparamita*.
4. The perfection of efforts, which is called *viryaparamita*.
5. The perfection of meditative absorption, which is called *dhyanaparamita*.
6. The perfection of wisdom, which is called *prajñāpāramitā*.
7. The perfection of skillful means, which is called *upayaparamita*.
8. The perfection of aspiration, which is called *pranidhanaparamita*.
9. The perfection of powers, which is called *balaparamita*.
10. The perfection of knowledge or wisdom, which is called *jñāna paramita*.

We must strive toward perfection in these different aspects of being. As mentioned above, we must strive to perfect our generosity or sense of sharing, giving without expectation of return. We must be morally ethical. We must practice patience, the right effort, meditativeness, etc.

Doing so, we will attain true and lasting/enduring enlightened happiness or bliss.

TEN FACTORS WHICH KEEP US AWAY FROM BLISS

Buddhism describes in detail ten unwholesome causes of action that keep us away from finding true bliss or happiness in life. These ten unwholesome causes of action are called the principles of the *akushala-karmapatha* in Sanskrit, *mi dge ba* in Tibetan, and *e yedao* in Chinese. They must be avoided at all costs if we seek to live in happiness.

These factors are:

1. Causing physical harm or killing others, i.e., *pranatipata*
2. The act of stealing, i.e., *adattadana*
3. Sexual misdemeanor, i.e., *kamamithyachara*
4. Telling lies, i.e., *mrishavada*
5. Harmful or malicious speech, i.e., *paishunyavada*.

6. Verbal abuse, i.e., *parushyavada*.
7. Frivolous talk or gossip, i.e., *sambhinnapralapa*.
8. Covetousness, i.e., *abhidhya*.
9. Having ill will or malice toward others, i.e., *vyapada*.
10. Cultivating wrongful views, i.e., *mithyadrishti*.

If we avoid these ten unwholesome causes of action, we will move toward blissfulness naturally. We must be mindful of avoiding these acts.

DISCOVERING TRUE BLISS: THE BUDDHA'S EIGHTFOLD NOBLE PATH

The most direct way to finding true bliss and happiness in life is to follow the Buddha's eightfold noble path, which is called *aryashtangamarga* in Sanskrit, *lam yan lag brgyad* in Tibetan, and *bazhengdao* or *bashengdao* in Chinese.

If we follow each of these eight teachings on the noble path, we attain a very deep blissfulness, which is not dependent on any material factors. The eightfold path of the Buddha comprises the cultivation of eight qualities:

1. Right Views or *Samyakdrishti.*
2. Right Intention or *Samyaksamkalpa.*
3. Right Speech or *Samyagvak.*
4. Right Action or *Samyakkarmanta.*
5. Right Livelihood or *Samyagajiva.*
6. Right Effort or *Samyagvyayama.*
7. Right Mindfulness or *Samyaksmriti.*
8. Right Concentration or *Samyaksamadhi.*

Focusing on each of these points of the eightfold path, we must understand that we are to align our consciousness to their teachings. For example, cultivating the right views and right intentions, moderating speech, putting our effort toward meditativeness, focusing ourselves on the right effort, and so on. If we follow these master keys of the Buddha, we attain spontaneous joy in life.

OM TARE TUTTARE TURE SVAHA
OM MANI PADME HUM

Acknowledgments

I would like to express my sincere gratitude to the individuals who have played a pivotal role in bringing this series to life: Anuj Bahri, my exceptional literary agent at Red Ink; Gaurav Sabharwal and Shantanu Duttagupta, my outstanding publishers at Fingerprint! Publishing, along with their dedicated team. Special thanks to Shilpa Mohan, my editor for her invaluable contributions.

I would also like to extend my heartfelt appreciation to my parents, Anita and Captain Jeet Gupta, for their unwavering support throughout this journey. To my beloved sister, Priti and brother-in-law, Manish Goel, thank you for always being there for me. My niece, Vaanee and nephew, Kartikay, have been a constant source of joy and inspiration and I am grateful for their presence in my life.

I am truly humbled by the collective efforts and encouragement from all these remarkable individuals, without whom this series would not have been possible.

Pranay is a renowned mystic, captivating speaker and accomplished author who has dedicated his life to exploring the depths of spirituality. With a deep understanding of the human experience and an unwavering commitment to personal growth, Pranay has written numerous books that offer insights into the realms of spirituality.

One of Pranay's most celebrated contributions is his groundbreaking series of modules titled "Advanced Spirituality for Leadership and Success." His transformative PowerTalks and MysticTalks have garnered international recognition for their exceptional ability to inspire and empower individuals from all walks of life. Pranay's unique approach combines ancient wisdom with contemporary insights, providing a roadmap for achieving spiritual fulfillment while embracing leadership qualities that lead to remarkable success.

To learn more about Pranay and his transformative teachings, visit his official website at pranay.org.

**To buy more books by the author
scan the QR code given below.**